DOG ON A LOG®
Chapter Books
Step 1

DOG ON A LOG Books
Tucson, Arizona

Public Domain images from
www.clker.com

ISBN: 978-1949471007

www.dogonalogbooks.com

FIVE
CHAPTER BOOKS
1

(A Collection of Five Books)

By Pamela Brookes

Download DOG ON A LOG printable gameboards, games, flashcards, and other activities at:
www.dogonalogbooks.com/printables.

Parents and Teachers:
Receive email notifications of new books and printables. Sign up at:
www.dogonalogbooks.com/subscribe

Table of Contents

DOG ON A LOG
Parent and Teacher Guides

General information
on Dyslexia and
Struggling Readers

The Author's Routine
for Teaching Reading

Book 1. *Teaching a Struggling Reader: One Mom's Experience with Dyslexia*

Book 2. *How to Use Decodable Books to Teach Reading*

Available for free from many online booksellers or read at:
www.dogonalogbooks.com/free

THE DOG
ON THE LOG

A Bit of a Pup

The dog is on a log. He is a bit of a dog. He is a pup.

The pup has a kid. His kid is a gal. His kid is Jan.

The dog is on a log.

To the Dam

"Tup," Jan says to the dog. "You are my pup. Let us hop."

Tup does wag.

"Let us go to the dam," Jan says.

They hop and run and hop to the dam. The sun is hot. Jan is hot. Tup is hot.

Jan Is Wet

At the dam, Jan says, "Let us get wet."

Hop, hop, hop. Jan is wet.

Tup does not want to get wet. He does not like to be wet. He can see Jan is wet and she is OK.

Jan is wet.

Tup Is Wet

Tup's leg is wet. He does not like that. Hop! Hop to the rock. His leg is not wet.

"You are OK. It is OK to be wet. You can get wet," Jan says.

Tup's back leg is wet. He does not like to be wet.

Tup's back leg is wet. He does not like to be wet.

"You are OK," Jan says.

Jan is wet. Her leg is wet. Her back is wet. Her neck is wet. She is OK.

If Jan can get wet, Tup can get wet. He does not want to get wet.

The Fish

Tup can see a fish. It is a big fish. A big red fish. Hop, hop, hop, to the fish. His leg is wet. His back is wet. His chin is wet. His neck is wet. He is wet, wet, wet.

This is fun!

He is wet, wet, wet. This is fun!

Hop, hop, hop to Jan. She is wet. Tup is wet. The big red fish is wet.

This is fun!

A pup.

A dog.

Sight Words used in "THE DOG ON THE LOG"

a, and, are, be, does, go, goes, has, he, her, his, into, is, like, my, of, OK, says, see, she, the, they, to, want, you

Approximately 260 total words

THE PIG HAT

The Hat

Sam got a hat with a dot on it. A big red dot.

He got the hat for his pig. His pig is Pam. She is a big pig. She is a big, fat pig.

His pig is Pam. She is a big pig. She is a big, fat pig.

The Hot Sun

Pam does not like the sun. It is hot. Pam does not like the hot sun.

Pam sees Sam. She does run to him. She does lick him. She does like him.

Sam does set the hat on Pam. The hat with the red dot.

The hat is on the pig. The sun is not on Pam. She is not hot.

The hat is on the pig.

The Jog

"You are not hot. Can we go for a jog?" says Sam.

Sam and Pam jog. They jog to the shop. It is a pig shop. "I can get you a pig yum," Sam says.

Sam and Pam jog.

Pam goes in the pig shop with Sam.

No Pig in The Shop

"That pig can not be in here," the shop gal says.

Pam is sad.

"I want to get her a pig yum," Sam says.

"That pig can not be in here," the shop gal says.

"You can get her a pig yum. That is OK. She can not be in the shop. It is not OK for her to be in the shop," the shop gal says.

Not in The Shop

"Can Pam the pig sit on the rug?" Sam says.

"The rug is in the shop. She can not sit on the rug," the shop gal says.

"Can she sit in your van? It is not in the shop," Sam says.

"I do not have a van," the shop gal says. "I do have a hot rod. She can sit in the hot rod."

"She can sit in the hot rod."

The Hot Rod

Sam goes to the hot rod with Pam. "You sit in the hot rod. I can get you a pig yum," Sam says.

Pam is in the hot rod. It is a red hot rod. She sees ick in the hot rod. She has a lick of the ick. Then she has a big lick of the ick.

"Pam, do not lick the hot rod," Sam says. "I got you a pig yum. You can lick it."

Pam is in the hot rod.

Pam has a lick of the pig yum. Then she has a big lick.

The Shop Gal

The shop gal has a pop for Sam.

"Pam did lick the ick in my hot rod. She can be in my hot rod. This yum bag is for Pam."

Pam does like the shop gal.

This yum bag is for Pam.

Pam does like Sam.

Pam does like her Pig Yum.

Sight Words used in
"The Pig Hat"

a, and, are, be, do, does, for, go, goes, has, have, he, her, here, his, I, like, my, no, of, says, sees, she, the, they, to, want, we, you, your

Approximately 400 total words

CHAD THE CAT

Bam on the Rug

Liz has a cat. Her cat is Chad. Chad is her pal.

Chad is on Liz's neck. "Chad, do you want a nap? You can nap in the box," Liz says.

Chad is on Liz's neck.

Chad does hop from Liz's neck. It is a bad hop. He goes bam on the rug. He hit his chin. He bit his lip. He cut his leg.

Get Mom

Liz and Chad sit. "Are you OK?" Liz says.

Chad does not nod. He is sad.

He is sad.

"Let me get Mom," Liz says. She goes to Mom. "Chad bit his lip and cut his leg."

"Let us go to Chad. Let us see his cut," Mom says.

To the Vet

"Are you OK?" Mom says to Chad. "Let us go see the vet. She can fix you up."

They get in the van. Chad is on Liz's lap. His chin is on her leg. He is sad.

They get in the van.

Fix Him Up

The vet is a gal. She has on a red top. "I can fix his chin. I can fix his lip. I can fix his cut leg," the vet says.

Liz does pet Chad. "The vet can fix you up. Do not be sad," Liz says.

The vet is a gal.

Sit and Sit

"Here is a shot for Chad. It can get him to nap. I can fix him up when he does nap. You can sit when I fix him up," the vet says.

Liz and her mom sit. They sit and sit and sit. Liz is in her mom's lap. Liz is up. She goes hop, hop, hop. Then she and Mom sit and sit.

Liz and her mom sit. They sit and sit and sit.

Fix Him

"I did fix Chad," the vet says. "I did fix his chin. I did fix his lip. I did fix the cut on his leg."

"Yes!" Liz says.

"He can go with you," the vet says. "He can not get on your neck. It is not OK if he goes bam."

"*He can go with you,*" the vet says.

Liz's Lap

Mom, Liz, and Chad get in the van. Chad is not sad. Chad is on Liz's lap. He does not get on Liz's neck. He has a nap in her lap.

Sight Words used in "CHAD THE CAT"

a, and, are, be, do, does, for, from, go, goes, he, her, here, I, me, of, OK, says, see, she, the, they, to, want, you, your

Approximately 340 total words

ZIP THE BUG

Zip Has A Nap

Zip the bug had a nap. He had a nap in his mug. Then the sun was up.

He had a nap in his mug.

Mug in The Sun

Zip's mug is in the sun. His mug is hot. Zip is hot.

Hop, hop, hop. He is not in his mug. Hop, hop, hop. He is on the rug.

He is on the rug.

Tag

Tag is Zip's pal. Tag is a big bug. He is a big bug with a red dot.

Tag is on the rug. Zip sees his pal. "Let us go get Jot," Zip says. "Then we can have fun."

Tag is Zip's pal.

The Rug

Zip and Tag hop on the rug. The sun is on the rug. The rug is hot, hot, hot.

"It is hot," Tag says.

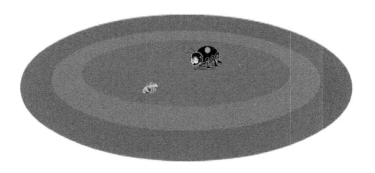

Zip and Tag hop on the rug. The sun is on the rug.

"Yes, and the rug is big. We have to hop a lot. We have to hop a lot to get to Jot," Zip says.

The Cat Dish

They hop to the cat dish. The dish is on a mat. The mat is wet. The cat got it wet. They do not see the cat. The cat is bad if you are a bug.

They hop to the cat dish.

The Web

They hop from the dish mat. They see a web. A web is bad if you are a bug. They do not see Jot in the web.

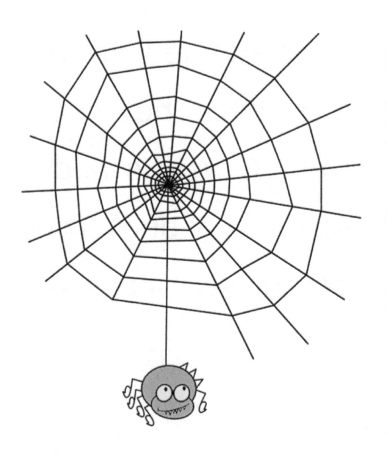

They see a web.

The Log

They go to the tub. Jot is not in the tub. A bug in a tub is bad. A bug in a tub can get wet.

They see a log. Jot is on the log. "Do you want to be on the log?" he says to Zip and Tag.

Zip, Tag, and Jot get on the log. It is fun.

Zip, Tag, and Jot go on the log.

Sight Words used in "ZIP THE BUG"

a, and, are, be, do, from, go, have, he, his, is, says, see, sees, the, they, want, was, we, you

Approximately 285 total words

THE FISH
AND THE PIG

The Fish Has A Pal

Val is a fish. Val has a pal. Her pal is a pig. The pig is Pam. "Do not sit here Pam. It is wet," the fish says to the pig.

"It is OK. I want to be here with you," the Pig says. "I want to sit with you. I have to get wet."

I want to sit with you .

The Wet Pig

Val the fish does not like that her pal is wet. Pam has a mud pen. Pam does like to be in the mud. She does not like to get wet.

"Let us see if we can sit and you not get wet," Val says.

"I have to get wet if I sit with you. That is OK," Pam says.

The Man

"Can the man get us a jug?" the fish says to the pig.

"A jug? You want a jug?" Pam says.

"Yes. A jug I can sit in," Val says.

"Can the man get us a jug?" the fish says
to the pig.

"If you are in a jug, the cat can nip you. I do not want the cat to nip you," Pam says.

A Jug?

Val and Pam sit. Pam is Val's pal.

Val is sad. She does not like Pam to be wet.

"You do not like to be wet. I am sad when you are wet. Can you see if the man has a jug?" Val says.

"I do not want you to be sad. What do you want the jug to be like?" Pam says.

"A jug that I can be in. A jug that I can be wet in," the fish says.

The Man in The Hat

The pig goes to the man. This man got Pam a hat. She likes her hat. The sun does not get Pam hot if she has her hat on.

The man has on Pam's hat.

The man has on Pam's hat.

The man is at his dish tub. He has his cup in the tub.

"Do you want your hat, Pam? Do you want to jog?" the man says.

The Jug

Pam sees a jug. She goes to the jug. Her lip is on the jug. She has the jug.

The man sees Pam with the jug, "Do not run with my jug," he says.

Pam goes to the fish with the jug.

She has the jug.

Get In

Pam is at the fish. "Here, get in the jug," Pam says.

Val does hop into the jug. She is wet.

With a tug and a tug Pam has the jug in her mud pen. Val and Pam sit. Pam is not wet.

Val is in the jug.

The Mud Pen

The man is in the mud pen. He sees the fish in the jug. He sees the pig sit with her pal.

"This is bad," the man says. "That jug is not big. Let me see if I have a big jug for the fish."

He sees the fish in the jug. He sees the pig
sit with her pal.

The Big Jug

The man has a big jug. It is a big, big jug. "Here you are," he says. "You can be in a big jug, Val. You can be with your pal. Pam, you can sit in the mud pen. You can sit and not get wet."

You can be in a big jug, Val.

The fish and the pig sit. The fish has a pal. Her pal is not wet.

Sight Words used in "THE FISH AND THE PIG"

a, and, are, be, do, does, for, goes, has, have, he, her, here, his, I, like, me, my, of, OK, says, see, sees, she, the, they, to, want, we, what, you, your

Approximately 470 total words

Excerpt from Step 2:
Mud on the Path

Step 2
- Bonus letters (f, l, s, z after short vowel)
- "all"
- –s suffix

Step 2 New Sight Words
could, do, eggs, for, from, have, here, I, likes, me, nest, onto, or, puts, said, say, sees, should, wants, was, we, what, would, your

Bob the Dog

Bob is a big dog. A big tan dog. He can pick up thick logs. He can sit and set his chin on the bed. He can get in the back of the van when he wants.

Bob is my pal. If I am sad, he will kiss my chin. He will get the ball when I toss it. He sits on the rug with me. I rub his back and neck.

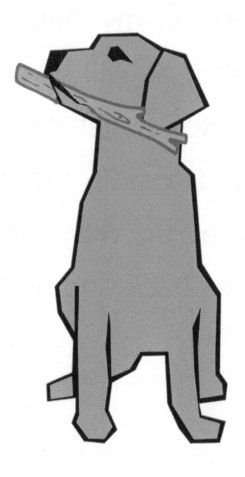

Bob is a big dog.

The Log Hut

Dad said Bob and I could pick up logs. I would pick up a log. Bob would jog with it to Dad. Dad cut the logs. He set log on top of log. Then he fit the logs with pegs. The logs got tall.

The logs are a hut. The hut is for me and Bob. The log hut is in the dip in the hills. The hut has a top. It can not get wet in the hut.

Step 2 Books
- Mud on the Path
- The Red Hen
- The Hat and Bug Shop
- Babs the 'Bot
- The Cub

KEYWORDS

Alphabet

Aa	Bb
apple	bat
Cc	Dd
cat	dog

Ee	Ff
Ed	fun
Gg	Hh
game	hat
Ii	Jj
itch	jug

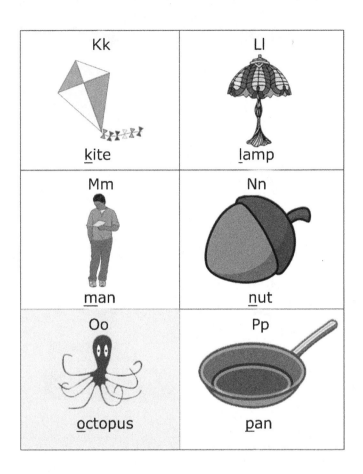

Kk	Ll
kite	lamp
Mm	Nn
man	nut
Oo	Pp
octopus	pan

Qu qu queen	Rr rat
Ss snake	Tt top
Uu up	Vv van

Ww	Xx
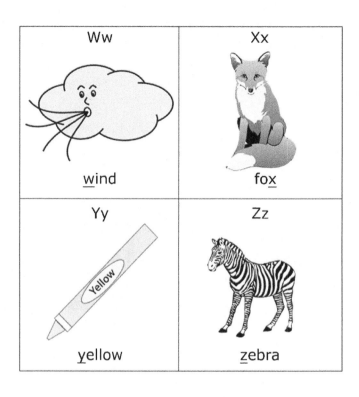	
_wind	fo_x
Yy	Zz
_yellow	_zebra

Digraphs

ch	sh
<u>ch</u>in	<u>sh</u>ip
th	th
<u>th</u>umb	mo<u>th</u>er
wh	-ck
<u>wh</u>istle	so<u>ck</u>

Phonics Progression

DOG ON A LOG Pup Books

Book 1

Phonological/Phonemic Awareness:

- Words
- Rhyming
- Syllables, identification, blending, segmenting
- Identifying individual letter sounds

Books 2-3

Phonemic Awareness/Phonics

- Consonants, primary sounds
- Short vowels
- Blending
- Introduction to sight words

DOG ON A LOG Let's GO! and Chapter Books

Step 1

- Consonants, primary sounds
- Short vowels
- Digraphs: ch, sh, th, wh, ck
- 2 and 3 sound words
- Possessive 's

Step 2

- Bonus letters (f, l, s, z after short vowel)
- "all"
- −s suffix

Step 3

- Letter Buddies: ang, ing, ong, ung, ank, ink, onk, unk

Step 4

- Consonant blends to make 4 sound words
- 3 and 4 sound words ending in −lk, -sk

Step 5

- Digraph blend −nch to make 3 and 4 sound words
- Silent e, including "-ke"

Step 6

- Exception words containing: ild, old, olt, ind, ost

Step 7

- 5 sounds in a closed syllable word plus suffix -s (crunch, slumps)
- 3 letter blends and up to 6 sounds in a closed syllable word (script, spring)

Step 8

- Two-syllable words with 2 closed syllables, not blends (sunset, chicken, unlock)

Step 9

- Two-syllable words with all previously introduced sounds including blends, exception words, and silent "e" (blacksmith, kindness, inside)
- Vowel digraphs: ai, ay, ea, ee, ie, oa, oe (rain, play, beach, tree, pie, boat, toe)

WATCH FOR MORE STEPS COMING SOON

Let's GO! Books
have less text

Chapter Books
are longer

DOG ON A LOG Books
Sight Word Progression

DOG ON A LOG Pup Books
a, does, go, has, her is, of, says, the, to

DOG ON A LOG Let's GO! and Chapter Books

Step 1
a, and, are, be, does, go, goes, has, he, her, his, into, is, like, my, of, OK, says, see, she, the, they, to, want, you

Step 2
could, do, eggs, for, from, have, here, I, likes, me, nest, onto, or, puts, said, say, sees, should, wants, was, we, what, would, your

Step 3
as, Mr., Mrs., no, put, their, there, where

Step 4
push, saw

Step 5
come, comes, egg, pull, pulls, talk, walk, walks

Step 6
Ms., so, some, talks

Step 7
Hmmm, our, out, Pop E., TV

Step 8
Dr., friend, full, hi, island, people, please

More DOG ON A LOG Books

Most books available in Paperback, Hardback, and e-book formats

DOG ON A LOG Parent and Teacher Guides

Book 1 (Also in FREE e-book and PDF Bookfold)
- Teaching a Struggling Reader: One Mom's Experience with Dyslexia

Book 2 (FREE e-book and PDF Bookfold only)
- How to Use Decodable Books to Teach Reading

DOG ON A LOG Pup Books
Book 1
- Before the Squiggle Code (A Roadmap to Reading)

Books 2-3
- The Squiggle Code (Letters Make Words)
- Kids' Squiggles (Letters Make Words)

DOG ON A LOG Let's GO! and Chapter Books

Step 1
- The Dog on the Log
- The Pig Hat
- Chad the Cat
- Zip the Bug
- The Fish and the Pig

Step 2
- Mud on the Path
- The Red Hen
- The Hat and Bug Shop
- Babs the 'Bot
- The Cub

Step 3
- Mr. Bing has Hen Dots
- The Junk Lot Cat
- Bonk Punk Hot Rod
- The Ship with Wings
- The Sub in the Fish Tank

Step 4
- The Push Truck
- The Sand Hill
- Lil Tilt and Mr. Ling
- Musk Ox in the Tub
- The Trip to the Pond

Step 5
- Bake a Cake
- The Crane at the Cave
- Ride a Bike
- Crane or Crane?
- The Swing Gate

Step 6
- The Colt
- The Gold Bolt
- Hide in the Blinds
- The Stone Child
- Tolt the Kind Cat

Step 7
- Quest for A Grump Grunt
- The Blimp
- The Spring in the Lane
- Stamp for a Note
- Stripes and Splats

Step 8
- Anvil and Magnet
- The Mascot
- Kevin's Rabbit Hole
- The Humbug Vet and Medic Shop
- Chickens in the Attic

Step 9
- Trip to Cactus Gulch 1: The Step-Up Team
- Trip to Cactus Gulch 2: Into the Mineshaft
- Play the Bagpipes
- The Hidden Tale 1: The Lost Snapshot

All chapter books can be purchased individually or with all the same-step books in one volume.

Steps 1-5 can be bought as Let's GO! Books which are less text companions to the chapter books.

All titles can be bought as chapter books.

WATCH FOR MORE BOOKS COMING SOON

How You Can Help

Parents often worry that their child (or even adult learner) is not going to learn to read. Hearing other people's successes (especially when they struggled) can give worried parents or teachers hope. I would encourage others to share their experiences with products you've used by posting reviews at your favorite bookseller(s) stating how your child benefitted from those books or materials (whether it was DOG ON A LOG Books or another book or product.) This will help other parents and teachers know which products they should consider using. More than that, hearing your successes could truly help another family feel hopeful. It's amazing that something as seemingly small as a review can ease someone's concerns.

DOG ON A LOG Quick Assessment

Have your child read the following words. If they can't read every word in a Step, that is probably where in the series they should start. Get a printable assessment sheet at: www.dogonalogbooks.com/how-to-use/ assessment-tool/

Step 1
fin, mash, sock, sub, cat, that, Dan's

Step 2
less, bats, tell, mall, chips, whiff, falls

Step 3
bangs, dank, honk, pings, chunk, sink, gong, rungs

Step 4
silk, fluff, smash, krill, drop, slim, whisk

Step 5
hunch, crate, rake, tote, inch, mote, lime

Step 6
child, molts, fold, hind, jolt, post, colds

Step 7
strive, scrape, splint, twists, crunch, prints, blend

Step 8
finish, denim, within, bathtub, sunset, medic, habit

Step 9
hundred, goldfinch, free, wheat, inhale, play, Joe

Made in the USA
Las Vegas, NV
01 November 2022

58541972R00083